T0128489

A DAILY DOSE OF
SUNSHINE

BREAKING DOWN GOD'S WORD TO APPLY TO DAILY LIVING

SANDY N. WARD, M.ED

authorHOUSE®

AuthorHouse™
1663 Liberty Drive
Bloomington, IN 47403
www.authorhouse.com
Phone: 1 (800) 839-8640

Published by AuthorHouse 04/30/2020

ISBN: 978-1-7283-6030-0 (sc)
ISBN: 978-1-7283-6029-4 (e)

Library of Congress Control Number: 2020907787

Print information available on the last page.

Dedicated to my best friend and late husband Gregory L. Ward, to my children Saron, Savon, and Sania, to my family and friends for their continued support!

Opening Prayer

Dear God,

I pray that every hand that touches this book and reads these words would be blessed and find favor with you. Give them your anointing. Provide them with clarity of your word and how it applies to their life. Strengthen these your people. Encourage their hearts. Lord you know every area of their life that is in need of a special touch from you. You have all power in your hands so release your healing power. Heal them in every area of their life. Heal their emotions, finances, families, bodies, and renew their thinking. Lord, have your way in their lives. Let them be made a better person because of their relationship with you. Lastly Father, allow everyone that they encounter to be made a better person and be blessed because of their presence. You oh Lord are mighty so our trust is in you. May the words on these pages be life changing and uplifting so that someone will be encouraged and improve their walk with you.

Amen

A Safe Hiding Place

PSALM 37:40 NIV

The LORD helps them and delivers them; he delivers them from the wicked and saves them, because they take refuge in him.

New Hood Translation:

There is nothing too hard for God. He sits high and looks low. He already knows all of your troubles and worries so you can cast them on him. Talk to God. Have you ever played hide and seek? Sometimes a person can hide so good that you have to call their name and command them to come out because nobody can find them. That's how it is when we rest in our father's arms. He will protect you, cover you, and hide you in times of trouble. Refuge refers to a secret hiding place, shelter, and safety. When times get hard like they are right now don't worry, God said he would hide you, and deliver you. Yes hard times can still come. Sickness will still be present but it will not overtake you. God has your back IF you choose to allow him to be your safe place. Keep trusting! Keep praying! Keep pushing!

Living Your Best Life

JEREMIAH 5: 7 NIV

"Why should I forgive you? Your children have forsaken me and sworn by gods that are not gods. I supplied all their needs, yet they committed adultery and thronged to the houses of prostitutes. 10 "Go through her vineyards and ravage them, but do not destroy them completely.21 Hear this, you foolish and senseless people, who have eyes but do not see, who have ears but do not hear.

New Hood Translation:

In Chapter 5 of Jeremiah the people of Jerusalem were living their best lives. Turn down for what? They were breaking Gods commandments, picking up prostitutes, worshiping idol Gods, lying, backsliding, and refusing to repent. After being given an opportunity to get it together and refusing God said enough. He commanded destruction to get their attention. He sent extensive damage and suffering. God is not to mocked. He said I have told you but you don't listen. I have shown you the way but you refuse to see. Now I will get your attention. You can not live a reckless life that is displeasing to God and think that there will be no consequences. It's time for the people of God to repent, pray, and seek God's face. Keep trusting! Keep praying! Keep pushing!

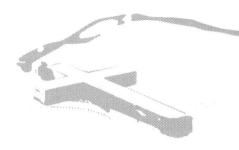

Actions speak louder than words

In the same way, let your light shine before others, that they may see your good deeds and glorify your Father in heaven.

New Hood Translation:

Actions are louder than words. You can not tell me one thing but show me another. How can you say God is good but you complain all the time? How can you say you trust God but you get nervous and doubt every time hard times come? The world weighs your actions much heavier than your words. Do people see Christ in you? Are they made better because of your presence? One thing I loved about my husband was I never wondered if he loved me because not only did he tell me but he showed me in every aspect that he could. People watch the way you react to different circumstances to see how you really feel. Now is not the time to worry. It's not the time to doubt. God is in control. Let the God in you shine light and offer encouragement to someone else. Keep trusting. Keep praying. Keep pushing!

Obedience Brings Blessings

DUET. 30:16 NIV

For I command you today to love the Lord your God, to walk in obedience to him, and to keep his commands, decrees and laws; then you will live and increase, and the Lord your God will bless you in the land you are entering to possess.

New Hood Translation:

It cost to be the boss. There is a price tag associated with being on top. Many times, we look at the life and lifestyles of others and wonder why we are lacking or still waiting for our blessing. You must be obedient to unlock your blessings. You can not live a reckless life and walk outside of the will of God and assess all he has in store for you. God already has blessings with your name on it but he said you have to obey me, love me (have relationship with me), and keep my commandments and THEN I will bless you. One-time Sam (my oldest brother) snuck in the closet and checked out our Christmas gifts early and because he did we had to wait a whole extra year until the next Christmas to get our

Nintendo. The gift was ours. It had already been assigned and purchased for us but his disobedience delayed all of our access. Don't delay your blessings! Keep trusting. Keep praying. Keep pushing!

Sit Down Somewhere

PSALM 46:10 NIV

Be still and know that I am God.

New Hood Translation:

Do not get caught up in everything that is going on around you. Things in this world will look scary but keep your eyes on God. Don't get caught up in the gossip. Stay calm. God will not led you to a place where he hadn't already made provisions for you to have a way out. You don't have to worry. Find a quiet place and turn to God's word. In Luke chapter 8 the disciples panicked and woke God because the storm was ragging and they feared they would die. Not only did God calm the sea but he said where is your faith? Do not get in an uproar because things look chaotic. Relax. God is still God. He will still heal. He will still protect and provide. He has all power in his hands. You just be still, stand on his word, and know that he is God. Keep trusting. Keep praying. Keep pushing!

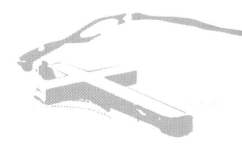

It's Not the Time to Doubt

PROVERBS 3:5 NIV

Trust in the Lord with all your heart and lean not on your own understanding.

New Hood Translation:

There are somethings that you will not be able to figure out. Even if you try to figure it out it still won't make sense to you and that's because God's ways are not our ways. He is beyond our thinking. We only see the pieces to the puzzle but he knows the finished product. Many people believe in God, that's the easy part but trusting his plan is where it gets difficult. When we see things falling apart we begin to doubt. When God said trust me with ALL your heart that includes your finances, family, health, relationships, and worries. He is saying it won't make sense to you but trust that I am working it out for your good. Stop letting everything rattle your feathers. God got you so accept what he allows. Pray about everything and worry about nothing. Positive vibes only. Keep trusting. Keep praying. Keep pushing.

Stress will kill you

PHIL. 4:6 NIV

Do not be anxious about anything, but in every situation, by prayer and petition, with thanksgiving, present your requests to God.

New Hood Translation:

Stress is one of the number one silent killers. Worrying will not change anything. When you feel overwhelmed pray. When you feel anxious pray. Don't just pray but thank God for what he has done and what you are expecting him to do. Stop running to people because they can't fix it. Pray. God has angels already assigned to look after you. You access your help by telling God what you need. He already knows but he is waiting to hear from you. Breathe. Slow down. Relax. Pray. Place everything before God and let it go! Keep trusting. Keep praying. Keep pushing!

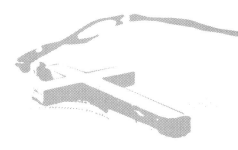

Dust your shoulders off

MATTHEW 10:14 NIV

If anyone will not welcome you or listen to your words, leave that home or town and shake the dust off your feet.

New Hood Translation:

Have you ever heard the saying don't beat a dead horse, wash your hands with it, or dust your shoulders off? It means to let it go and keep pushing. Sometimes you keep trying to save someone that doesn't want to be saved or you feel like your words are falling on deaf ears. Everyone will not be receptive to your words or godly advice. You just make sure the advice you are giving is actually godly. Some people will not like you no matter what you do. If they can't receive your words or reject you, shake the dust off your feet. Simply saying move around. It's my job to bring you the word of God but I cannot make you receive it and I can't make you love me. Stop getting caught up in people's opinion. Keep trusting! Keep praying. Keep pushing!

It's Part of the Plan

ROMANS 8:28 NIV

And we know that in all things God works for the good of those who love him, who have been called according to his purpose.

New Hood Translation:

Who said everyday would be blue skies and sunshine? Life happens. You can not control what will happen but you can control how you respond to the situation. Everything does not always go according to our plans. That's because God is in control and not us. He knows what lies ahead. When you walk with God and love him he ensures that everything falls in place for your protection and benefit. Even the things that look like setbacks and disappointments are part of his design. God will give us a no to block what was meant to harm us. He will close doors that lead down the wrong path. It doesn't matter what it looks like. It is working for your good. You have to trust the process, yes it can be disappointing but it is part of the plan and it is designed so you win. Stop tripping, it is no coincidence it is by design. Count it all joy. Keep trusting! Keep praying. Keep pushing!

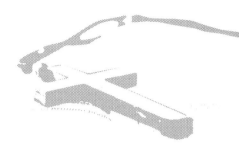

Change Your Thoughts

EPHESIANS 3:20 NKJV

Now to him who is able to do exceedingly abundantly beyond all that we ask or think, according to the power that works within us.

New Hood Translation:

Sometimes our blessings are held up because our thinking stinks. We get wrapped up in doubt and what ifs. God is prepared to blow your mind. He said he is able to do more than you could ever think or ask but what are you asking for? You have not because you ask not. What are your thoughts? It's time to move to next level thinking? You have blessings stored up with your name on it. It's time to access your blessings. That's why positive energy and people are so important. Your thoughts are powerful. I don't know about you but I am prepared for God to blow my mind. I don't want to just be blessed I want everything I touch and everything connected to me to be blessed. I expect my children, my grandchildren, and their children to be blessed for generations to come because of the prayers I prayed and the decisions I made. It's your season to win. It is time to get these exceedingly abundantly blessings flowing. Keep trusting! Keep praying. Keep pushing!

Why panic just pray?

PSALM 91:7 NIV

A thousand may fall at your side, ten thousand at your right hand, but it will not come near you.9 **If** you say, "The Lord is my refuge,"and you make the Most High your dwelling, 10 no harm will overtake you, no disaster will come near your tent.11 For he will command his angels concerning you to guard you in all your ways;

New Hood Translation:

Yes bad things will happen. Disease will outbreak. Plagues will arise. Cities will be in ruin. But God will take care of his children (**if** you trust him). That word "if" means under these conditions. **If** you believe that the Lord is your protection and your shelter in times of trouble then you go to sleep at night and know God will protect you. You will see disaster but it won't touch you. There are angels assigned to protect you. No you are not exempt from hard times, difficulties, or heartbreak but there is a shield of protection around you. You won't be overtaken. God is bigger than the Coronavirus or any other sickness. We don't live in fear because we stand on his promises. Washing your hands and covering your cough is great but you better learn how to plead the blood of Jesus over yourself and those around you and know no weapon formed against you shall prosper. We don't walk in panic we walk in peace. Read your word. Keep trusting! Keep praying. Keep pushing.

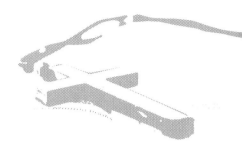

Encourage Yourself

David was greatly distressed because the men were talking of stoning him; each one was bitter in spirit because of his sons and daughters. But David found strength in the Lord his God.

Isaiah 41:10 NKJV

Fear not, for I am with you; be not dismayed for I am your God; I will strengthen you.

New Hood Translation:

It's wonderful to have a praying momma, an encouraging friend, or a motivating pastor but sometimes you have to encourage self. There will be times in life when you will slip in a rut for good reason and sometimes for no reason at all. The word said I will strengthen you. Stop looking for answers from people when God holds the answer to all of your problems. Sometimes you have to look yourself in the mirror and say you got this, no weapon formed against me will prosper, I choose to have joy, I can do all things through Christ who strengthens me. It is a blessing to have a support system but you have to know how to walk through the dark times knowing God holds your hand. You have to be your biggest fan. Cheer yourself on. You were created to win and designed for greatness. Better days are coming. Live, laugh, and love. Keep trusting! Keep praying! Keep pushing!

Stop Rushing Things

Be patient, then, brothers and sisters, until the Lord's coming. See how the farmer waits for the land to yield its valuable crop, patiently waiting for the autumn and spring rains.

New Hood Translation:

Have you ever bit into fruit and it's so sour it leaves a bitter taste in your mouth? Fruit is delicious but only in the right season. You can not rush God. He has already planned out your life. Just because you get in a rush doesn't make it happen. He knows what is best for you. Pray and praise him while you are waiting. Not even a tree can bear fruit until God says it's time and if it produces out of season it will be rotten. Don't spoil your blessings by trying to move in your own time. Ask God to help you align your will to his will. He knows the desires of your heart and he will bless you but in his time. No need to trip. God got you but you have to wait. Waiting patiently shows God you trust him.

Your gifts are already prewrapped. He just wants to make sure you are ready so you won't ruin it. Trust his timing! It's our season to win but you have to wait for it. Keep trusting! Keep praying. Keep pushing!

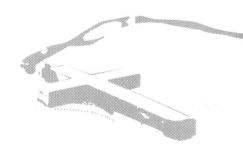

Just Trust God

MATTHEW 8: 24 NIV

Suddenly a furious storm came up on the lake, so that the waves swept over the boat. But Jesus was sleeping. 25 The disciples went and woke him, saying, "Lord, save us! We're going to drown!"26 He replied, "You of little faith, why are you so afraid?" Then he got up and rebuked the winds and the waves, and it was completely calm.

New Hood Translation:

Why worry? The same God that brought you out of the last storm will carry you through every trial. In these verses God had just finished performing miracles but the people still panicked when the storm arose. They couldn't understand how God could just lay there and sleep with a storm so fierce. God was saying wow do you still doubt me. Nothing can overtake you that God does not allow. Relax. Get some rest. It's in his hands. Even the winds and waves obey him. If you take your hands off of it then God will take over. He is just waiting for you to release it into his hands. There is nothing too hard for God. He sees your situation. He knows what you are going through. While you are talking about the problem he has already assigned the answer. He just wants to see if you will trust him. Keep trusting. Keep praying. Keep pushing!

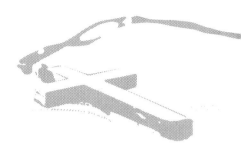

Forgive

EPH. 4:31 NIV

Get rid of all bitterness, rage and anger, brawling and slander, along with every form of malice. **32** Be kind and compassionate to one another, forgiving each other, just as in Christ God forgave you.

New Hood Translation:

Relax. Be careful the way you respond. Treat people how God treats you not how they treat you. This is a tough one. Our initial thought when someone wrongs us is to get them back, check them, or cut them loose. Stop allowing people and situations to get your blood boiling. Be slow to anger. God sends difficult people around so they can learn from you. I used to get angry and say Lord I want positive vibes around me only, why do you send me these difficult to deal with people. In my years of teaching I tend to get some of the lowest and worst behaved kids but it's because God trusts and knows that I can reach them and grow them.

It's the same reason he sends us difficult people so we can reach them and grow them. Don't give them a piece of your mind, give them Jesus. Trials come to make you strong. Keep trusting! Keep praying! Keep pushing!

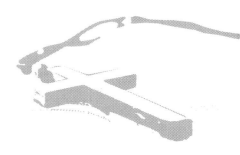

God's Plans

JEREMIAH 29:11 NIV

For I know the plans I have for you," declares the Lord, "plans to prosper you and not to harm you, plans to give you hope and a future.

New Hood Translation:

It won't always look how you want it to. It won't always happen like you want it to or when you want it to but trust God. He holds your future. He has preordained how and when things will happen. You can not rush or doubt God. If he said it that settles it. He will not put you in harms way. It doesn't matter what people say or what doors close. It may look like everyone around you is getting their blessing and promise quicker but God said they that wait upon the Lord shall renew their strength. Stand still and trust God. He has already wrote it into your future. Keep trusting! Keep praying. Keep pushing!

Count It All Joy

PHIL 4:11 NIV

I am not saying this because I am in need, for I have learned to be content whatever the circumstances.

New Hood Translation:

Count it all joy! Don't get shook up every time things happened. If you are going to trust God, then trust him. Take your hands off of it and know that he works all things out for your good. Learn to be at peace despite the situation because it's in God's hands. It could always be worst. God will not fail you. No matter what it looks like it will work out for your good. It's not a coincidence. God added it to your story because it is one of the puzzle pieces that will come together for your big picture. Thank God in spite of how it looks and hold on to your joy in every situation. Rejoice in the mist of the situation. Keep trusting! Keep praying. Keep pushing!

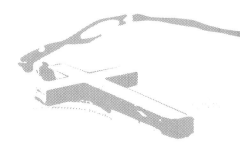

Watch How You Respond

PHIL. 1:27 NIV

Whatever happens, conduct yourselves in a manner worthy of the gospel of Christ. Then, whether I come and see you or only hear about you in my absence, I will know that you stand firm in the one Spirit, striving together as one for the faith of the gospel.

New Hood Translation:

You should know a tree by the fruit it bears. You can not flip out and act a fool in every situation. It is easy to lose your cool. It takes discipline to keep your cool. In everything you do people should see the God in you. You may be the only example of God they see. Before you respond to a person or situation consider if God would be pleased. People will continue to get under your skin if you allow them to. Every situation does not warrant a response from you. Your ability to walk away and pray about it will produce better results than you responding with words and actions that you can not take back. It is only a test. Keep trusting. Keep praying. Keep pushing!

Fear Not

ISAIAH 41:10 NKJV

Fear not, for I am with you; be not dismayed, for I am your God; I will strengthen you, I will help you, I will uphold you with my righteous right hand. "Do not be dismayed, for I am your God; I will strengthen you, I will help you, I will uphold you with my righteous right hand."

New Hood Translation:

Stop tripping. You have nothing to worry about. Don't stress yourself. I am God. I have all power. When you are weak I will give you strength. I got you. I have your back. People will love you today and leave you tomorrow but God won't fail. His love is unconditional. Stop troubling yourself because it's nothing too hard for God. God has already promised us protection and strength for difficult times. You have to exercise your faith and know that you will get through this. If God be for you, who can be against you? Keep trusting. Keep praying. Keep pushing!

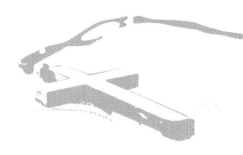

What about your friends?

MARK 2:3 NIV

Some men came, bringing to him a paralyzed man, carried by four of them. 4 Since they could not get him to Jesus because of the crowd, they made an opening in the roof above Jesus by digging through it and then lowered the mat the man was lying on. 5 When Jesus saw their faith, he said to the paralyzed man, "Son, your sins are forgiven."

New Hood Translation:

In Mark Chapter 2 versus 3-5 A paralyzed man was healed because of the faith of his friends. They were so determined to get their friend to Jesus that they bussed through the roof to bypass the crowd. The company you keep matters. Everybody that wears your jersey is not a fan. Some people will dog you out behind your back whispering how you will never change and applauding your failures while others will pray for your change, your healing, and carry you through ushering you to Jesus. Don't just look at your circle, look at yourself. What kind of friend are you? Are the people around you made better because of your presence? Positive vibes only. Keep trusting. Keep praying. Keep pushing.

Hard times will come

PSALM 34:18 NIV

The Lord is close to the brokenhearted and saves those who are crushed in spirit. 19 A righteous man may have many troubles but the Lord delivers him from the all;

New Hood Translation:

You will never know that God mends broken hearts if you have never had your heart broken. You will never know he provides if you haven't experienced lack. You are in this place intentionally. God is using you to not just get the glory but show someone else how to find light in darkness. God has the answer to every problem you are facing. Learn to thank God for joy during difficult times. God is good all the time. Rough days do occur but God shows up even on those days. Be grateful. It could always be worst. Keep trusting. Keep praying. Keep pushing!

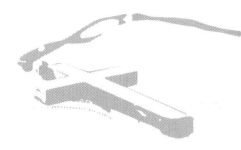

You are too close to give up

2 CHRONICLES 15:7 NIV

But as for you, be strong and do not give up, for your work will be rewarded.

New Hood Translation:

The only way you can lose is to forfeit the victory that has already been assigned to. God wants to heal where you hurt but it is some things you have to let go of. Protect your energy and let go of negative vibes. Take time for yourself and trust God to do what he said. You are closer to your breakthrough than you know. You did not come this far to give up. The enemy attacks you the hardest when he sees that you are close to the finish line. He knows if he can convince you to give up now you will miss the blessing that is right ahead of you. Now is the time to mustard up your strength and keep going. You will not lose. You were created for greatness. Keep trusting. Keep praying. Keep pushing!

You have a reason to be thankful

Give thanks to the Lord, for he is good; his love endures forever.

New Hood Translation:

Oh give thanks unto the Lord for he is good and his mercy endureth forever. Our situations are not always good but God is always good in the mist of everything we face. In this season of Thanksgiving let NOTHING distract you from being grateful for the many blessings after blessings that God keeps sending. He keeps providing. He keeps making a way. He keeps drying tears. Some days can represent hard times and can feel impossible to get through but still be grateful. Do not rob God of your praise because he is worthy! Be thankful! With a grateful heart give thanks for the many blessings you have already received and those yet to come. Keep trusting. Keep praying. Keep pushing!

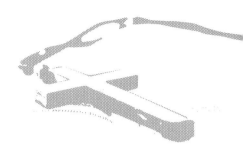

I Won't Complain

NUMBERS 11:1 NLV

Soon the people began to complain about their hardship, and the Lord heard everything they said. Then the Lord's anger blazed against them, and he sent a fire to rage among them, and he destroyed some of the people in the outskirts of the camp.

New Hood Translation:

When we complain we are telling God his work is not enough. We have to understand that although things look bad it could always be worst. Learn to count it all joy! We all get frustrated but let's walk in a spirit of thankfulness. Stop talking about it and start praying about it! We were promised that all things work together for our good. That includes the good, the bad, and the ugly. Things will not always go smoothly but the situation is still designed for God to get the glory. Hard times come to make you strong. It will get better. Stop complaining. Keep trusting. Keep praying. Keep pushing.

Don't Look Back

ISAIAH 46: 9 NIV

Remember the former things of old: for I am God, and there is none else; I am God, and there is none like me, 10 Declaring the end from the beginning, and from ancient times the things that are not yet done, saying, My counsel shall stand, and I will do all my pleasure:

New Hood Translation:

God has an appointed predestined plan for you. He is never late. Sometimes we get distracted by the circumstances of life and forget that God is in complete control. God shows us the plan through prayer. You can not get results because you are not putting in work. You have to build a relationship. When you need vision, you have to go to your maker. You wouldn't take your Apple iPhone to Samsung. Cast your cares on him. Stop running to people to get an answer to your problem. Do not worry about your past. God sent you through the fire but you will not smell like smoke. You will not look like what you have been through. Your best is yet to come! Keep trusting. Keep praying. Keep pushing!

Everybody Is Not Your Friend

ISAIAH 29:13 NIV

The Lord says: "These people come near to me with their mouth and honor me with their lips, but their hearts are far from me.

New Hood Translation:

Don't fall for the okie doke. Just because they wear your Jersey does not make them a fan or part of your team. Some people desire to get close to you because they see how God blesses you. They like your shine but can't wait for you to fall. When people talk against your name their words sow seed to your harvest. People will envy you because of the favor they see on your life. They do not understand why God blesses you the way that he does. Do not get discouraged when people speak against your name. Ask God to bless you to bless somebody else. Enjoy this beautiful day! Smile. Keep trusting. Keep praying. keep pushing!

It's Time to Grow Up

1 CORINTHIANS 13:11 NIV

When I was a child. I thought as a child but when I became a man, I put away childish things.

New Hood Translation:

I used to say anything and cared less how it came out. Now I think twice. Growth. Confidence grows when you learn to make peace with your past. Sometimes you have to look back over some of the things God let you go through so you can move confidently into your future. Greater is the God that is in you. You are not who people say you are. Choose to be better not bitter. Keep trusting. Keep praying. Keep pushing!

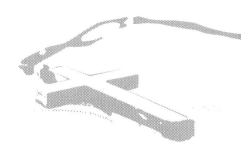

Count It All Joy

JAMES 1:2-3 NKJV

My brethren, count it all joy when you fall into various trials, knowing that the testing of your faith produces patience.

New Hood Translation:

How do we remain joyful in difficult times? Trusting God is easy when skies are blue and resources are plentiful. Hard times come to make us strong. Stop telling people how big your problems are and show them how big your God is. Stop wasting what God has blessed you with. You face trials to strengthen you. You face hard times to show you what you are made of. The trials test your faith but teach you how to trust God. It is a necessary part of the progress. Think of it as falling off of a bike when you are learning to ride. Yes it hurts but it does not mean you are not meant to ride a bike. It just teaches you how to balance and how to get back up and keep going. There may be some bumps in the road but they will only help you grow. Keep trusting. Keep praying. Keep pushing!

Get To Work

JAMES 2:26 NIV

As the body without the spirit is dead, so faith without deeds is dead.

New Hood Translation:

You can not conqueror what you don't confront. Sometimes we are waiting on God to move and he is waiting on us to move. Faith without works is dead. You have to do your part. It is time out for just sitting around waiting for blessings to fall in our lap. Faith means you are believing God for things you have yet to see. Work means get off your behind and make some things happen. God wants to see that you are ready for the blessing he is about to send your way. Sometimes we miss out because our hands are already full. You have to make room for God. Keep trusting. Keep praying. Keep pushing!

This too shall pass

JOHN 16:33 NIV

I have told you these things, so in me you may have peace. In this world you will have trouble. But take heart! I have overcome the world.

New Hood Translation:

God has already told us we will have hard times. Not we might. It's guaranteed. So stop tripping. Some times as children of God we feel like we should be exempt from the problems that others face. God never said we would be exempt but he promised that he would never leave us nor forsake us. That means yes you will face hard times but you will not have to face it alone. When you cry out to our Father, he will help you to overcome every difficulty. You will not have to face your battles alone and you can face them knowing that the hard times won't last. Trust and believe. Keep trusting. Keep praying. Keep pushing.

Sometimes You Have to Change Locations

"He brought me out into a spacious place; he rescued me because he delighted in me."

New Hood Translation:

Today take time to reflect on the weights you have in your life. It's hard to fly when you are being weighed down by negative energy in your life. God is preparing a special place for you and the door is waiting to be opened. Don't let the people in your life keep you outside in the wilderness, for the place god has for you is a place unimaginable and full of deliverance. God knows how to move you out of the way of confusion so he can get your attention. Some times he has to stir up some things in your life so he can get his glory. Trust the plan. It is meant for your good because he thinks so much of you. Don't get distracted, It is for the best. Keep trusting. Keep praying. Keep trusting!

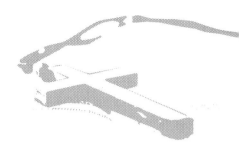

Stay Connected

JAMES 4:8 NIV

Come near to God and he will come near to you. Wash your hands, you sinners, and purify your hearts, you double-minded.

New Hood Translation:

Whenever you unplug a lamp no matter how good it works the power leaves. Stay connected to the source. God has all the power but you have to stay connected. Time to reconnect! Look to the hills from which cometh your strength. It is a season of breakthrough. No matter what decisions you may be facing today, God wants to equip you and empower you to make the right choices. The answer to every situation we face is addressed in God's Word either directly or by principle. Stay in the word of God. Keep Trusting. Keep praying. Keep pushing.

Your Best Is Yet To Come

1 CORINTHIANS 2:9 NKJV

Eyes have not seen, nor ears heard, nor have entered into the heart of man the things which God has prepared for those who love him.

New Hood Translation:

If you could see you're not yet, you would be shouting over your right now. Everybody in the bible that received tremendous blessing went through a rut before they got to promise. God is going to bless you to the point that even the enemies who attacked you will be blessed because they are around you. Sometimes it feels like you have been in this dark place too long. It's been a rut but God is preparing a new route. If you want to change your rut change your routine. Minor setbacks will not shake you. They are wonderful tools in God's hand to teach us. He will use them as opportunities to instruct and remove the enemy's plan to discourage us from the way he has chosen for us to walk. If God be for you who can be against you? Because God has given us the victory in the next chapter we walk through this section of the story with joy and great expectations. Keep trusting. Keep praying. Keep pushing.

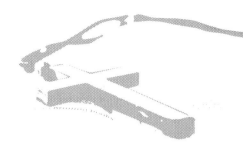

God Is With You

DUET. 31: 6 NIV

Be strong and courageous. Do not be afraid or terrified because of them, for the LORD your God goes with you; he will never leave you nor forsake you."

New Hood Translation:

Keep holding on. God is light to darkness. He will not fail you. You do not have to be worried. You can face every trial and storm that comes your way because God is with you. Put your faith and trust in him. We do not deserve his grace but he continues to provide for us. God has promised to be with us even until the end of the earth. You are never alone. No matter how big the problem is God is bigger than your situation. The enemy wants to convince you that this thing is going to take you out but I dare you to activate your faith. Trust God. You will not be defeated. Hold your head up. Keep trusting. Keep praying. Keep pushing!

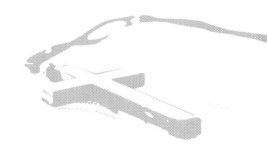

We Need Your Peace

PHIL 4:7 NIV

And the peace of God, which transcends all understanding, will guard your hearts and your minds in Christ Jesus.

New Hood Translation:

Father we need you now. We need your peace like never before. Right after verse 6 of Philippians when the Lord said don't worry about anything but pray about everything he then followed up by letting us know he would give us peace. So the equation is not worrying, a lot of praying, equals peace. His word said if we keep our minds on him, not on the news, not on our job, not on our concerns but on him, we would have peace. Most gracious father so much is rapidly occurring around us, fears are high, anxiety is high, but your word said we don't have to worry just pray. So father, we look to you. You already promised that the enemy would not devour us so we rest in you. We don't know what is to come but we know it's in your hands. Consume us with your peace in the mist of turbulent times. You said you wouldn't leave us nor forsake us so we rest knowing we are covered by your blood. Keep trusting. Keep praying. Keep pushing.

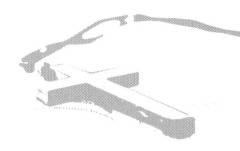

So much to be thankful for

Rejoice always, 17 pray continually, 18 give thanks in all circumstances; for this is God's will for you in Christ Jesus.

New Hood Translation:

How do you smile in the mist of turmoil? God is still good. He is still providing and making a way. Be of good cheer. Count it all joy! He gave us the blueprint.

1. Rejoice - Keep smiling, keep a positive attitude, and push through.

2. Pray – Don't stop praying. God knows all about your troubles and so make your request known to God.

3. Give Thanks - We don't wait for the problem to past. We thank God in the middle of it.

Father we thank you for providing All of our needs. Thank you for protecting our families. Thank you for keeping us together when we wanted to fall apart. Thank you for your goodness and mercy. We have some much to thank God for. Rejoice, pray, and give thanks.

Keep trusting. Keep praying. Keep pushing!

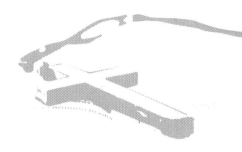

Separate Yourself

ISAIAH 26:20 NIV

Go, my people, enter your rooms and shut the doors behind you; hide yourselves for a little while until his wrath has passed by.

New Hood Translation:

God has all power in his hands. He is able to do all things. He can choose to save or destroy, to punish or reward. The decision is his. There are times when he calls us to separate. In order to be removed from sin, plague, and destruction he calls us to draw near to

him. God is commanding us to sit aside distraction. It's time to find a quiet place and spend time alone in his presence. The key to building relationships is quality time and communication. God is a jealous God. Spend this time strengthening your relationship with

him. Worship outweighs worry. Remember rejoice, pray, and give thanks. Keep trusting. Keep praying. Keep pushing!

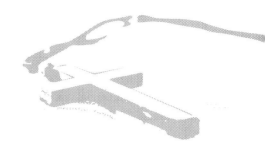

God is going to do it again

MARK 8:17 NIV

Aware of their discussion, Jesus asked them: "Why are you talking about having no bread? Do you still not see or understand? Are your hearts hardened? 18 Do you have eyes but fail to see, and ears but fail to hear? And don't you remember?

New Hood Translation:

God is the same today, tomorrow, and forever more. Do not forget what he has already brought you through. If he did it before he will do it again? In the book of Mark chapter 8 Jesus had just taken the little that they had and stretched it and supplied their needs by feeding the multitudes. Right after he blessed them the pharisees were already complaining about their lack and saying if you really have these powers send us a sign from Heaven. Jesus turned around like are you guys serious? Didn't you see what I just did? After I just blessed you and just made a way, and you saw me provide but you still doubt. You have eyes but can't see. Stop looking at what is before you with such distress. The same God that always supplies your needs will come through. It's not time to doubt. Rejoice, pray, and thank God. Keep trusting. Keep pushing. Keep praying!

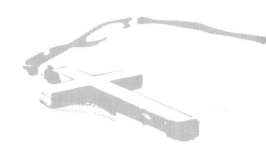

People are always watching

1 THESS. 3:7 NIV

Therefore, brothers and sisters, in all our distress and persecution we were encouraged about you because of your faith. 8 For now we really live, since you are standing firm in the Lord.

New Hood Translation:

We are facing tough and difficult times. There is great fear and worry around us. It seems like the news we are receiving is getting worse and worse. Situations changing by day but God has not changed. He still reigns. He still protects and provides. The earth belongs to the Lord. He is in control. Those around you are watching how you respond to the situation. They are encouraged by your faith. You could never exercise faith if you didn't face some impossible situations. During this time negative words are not needed. Somebody is depending on your encouragement. Allow your faith to uplift someone else. Father forgive our complaining and disbelief. Our hope and trust is in God. Keep trusting. Keep praying. Keep pushing.

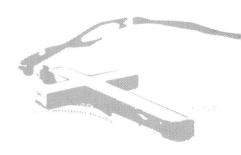

God is still good

PSALM 34:8 NIV

Taste and see that the Lord is good; blessed is the one who takes refuge in him.

New Hood Translation:

God is still on the throne. Times are hard, sickness is present, resources are limited but the God who supplies all of our needs is still good! Forget not his benefits. The same God who carried and kept you this far is still a way maker. He is still healing. He is still opening doors. He never said it would be easy. He promised us hard times but he promised to never leave us. His mercy is good. His grace is good. His hedge of protection is good. His ability to mend broken hearts is good. Oh taste and see that the Lord is good! I don't always feel good but the God I serve is still good all the time. Unleash your blessings by praising his name. Keep trusting. Keep praying. Keep pushing.

God is Bigger Than Your Problems

PSALM 3:3 NIV

But you, Lord, are a shield around me, my glory, the One who lifts my head high.4 I call out to the Lord, and he answers me from his holy mountain.

New Hood Translation:

Depression is real but so is God. Mental struggles can be a heavy burden but it is not a burden you have to carry alone. The enemy knows if he can get in your head he can impact your heart. God has promised us healing, protection, grace, and favor. He told us to be of good cheer and cast our cares upon him. Accept what he allows. Know that all things work together for your good. Life will not always feel good but God will still be good. He desires to heal you where you are hurting. God is the lifter of our heads. Be encouraged. It will get better. Everybody faces hard times but it is how you face them when they arise. Family and friends are important they can help you but they can't heal you. Call on the Lord. He has your answer. What are you thankful for? Keep trusting. Keep praying. Keep pushing!

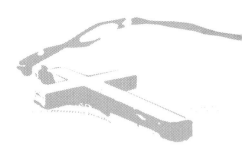

It will work out

MATTHEW 6:34 NIV

Therefore, do not worry about tomorrow, for tomorrow will worry about itself. Each day has enough trouble of its own.

New Hood Translation:

God never said do not make plans. He said do not worry. Focus on what is before you and make the best out of today. Worrying causes unneeded stress. Doubt delays your blessings. Trust and believe and make your requests known to God. Your steps are ordered. It's already worked out. Smile. Keep trusting. Keep praying. Keep pushing!

How bad do you want it?

JOHN 5:6 NIV

When Jesus saw him lying there and learned that he had been in this condition for a long time, he asked him, "Do you want to get well?"

New Hood Translation:

Stop complaining and put your faith to work. Now is not the time to walk in defeat. You have to keep a winning attitude and avoid

negative thinking and negative thinkers. In the book of John chapter 5 there was a pool where people were going to get healed but one man had been coming for 38 years anticipating healing and never been healed. The man complained because he was cripple and

the crowds always rushed passed him so he would miss his healing. Yes he couldn't walk but I often wonder why he didn't slide to the water, or roll to the water, grab somebody's ankle and be drug to the water. It's time out for excuses and watching everybody else get

blessed. You've got to get the right team and the right attitude. God is in the blessing business but how bad do you want it? It's time to get your finances in order, your family in order, your degree, your healing (physically, emotionally, mentally).You can not just nurse wounds you need to be willing to get up and fight for it. Do you want better? Keep trusting. Keep praying. Keep pushing!

We are not the same

JOHN 15:18 NIV

"If the world hates you, keep in mind that it hated me first. 19 If you belonged to the world, it would love you as its own. As it is, you do not belong to the world, but I have chosen you out of the world. That is why the world hates you.

New Hood Translation:

Everyone is not supposed to love you. Everyone did not love Jesus. There are some people that no matter what you do, there is just something about you that rubs them wrong. News Flash it is the holy spirit in you that annoys them. We have been commanded to be in this world but not of this world. Yes we reside here but God has assigned promises, provisions, and protection just for us. Has your parent ever said I don't care what they do, they are not my child? God says the same to us. You can't follow the led you most focus on the "leader". You were meant to be different. You can't respond how the world responds because you have a different covenant. Yes we face the same issues but we don't get the same results. God is still providing, still making ways, still opening doors, still keeping your family protected so your praise should be different. Look around. We are not the same. Rejoice because it could have been you. Pray so you will continue to be covered. Give thanks that in the mist of chaos and famine God is still protecting you. It's not time to panic now is the time to pray and praise. We are not the same! Keep trusting, keep praying, and keep pushing.

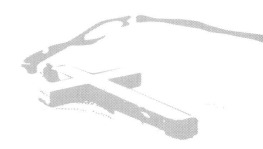

I Already Told You

JOSHUA 1:9 NIV

"Have I not commanded you? Be strong and courageous. Do not be terrified; do not be discouraged, for the Lord your God will be with you wherever you go."

New Hood Translation:

Life will happen. Every day will not be sunshine but God has already said don't sweat it. In the most difficult times be strong and face your difficulties with positive attitudes. In this chapter of Joshua, he was overwhelmed with fear. Repeatedly God reminded him that it doesn't matter what it looks like because I am with you. God is still with us. Yes it looks frightening but when there is nothing you can do then you must trust that God will handle it. God won't forsake you. It will work out. Keep trusting. Keep pushing. Keep praying.

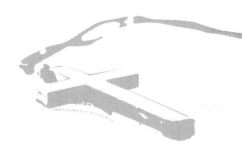

Do you believe?

MATT. 17:19 NIV

Then the disciples came to Jesus in private and asked, "Why couldn't we drive it out?"20 He replied, "Because you have so little faith. Truly I tell you, if you have faith as small as a mustard seed, you can say to this mountain, 'Move from here to there,' and it will move. Nothing will be impossible for you."

New Hood Translation:

The Coronavirus devastated our nation. It was not just attacking one country, one city, or one race. It attacked old and young, rich and poor, and all races. The molecules of the virus were invisible to the eye and that's what made it so powerful. We could not see it but it's powers were undeniable. How big is your faith? Is it bigger than that molecule? What about a mustard seed? You have to see it before you see it. Do you believe better days are coming? Do you believe God's protection is on you? God's perfect will is being performed. He is reuniting families, removing distractions, and testing faith. You don't have time to doubt in this season. It will delay your blessings. Read his word and then command blessings, protection, and healing over yourself and your house. No weapon formed will prosper. You have to continue walking in faith not fear! Keep trusting. Keep praying. Keep pushing!

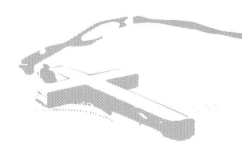

Just stand

EPHESIANS 6:13 NIV

Therefore, put on the full armor of God, so that when the day of evil comes, you may be able to stand your ground, and after you have done everything, to stand.

New Hood Translation:

What do you do when you don't know what to do? You trust God. You cover yourself in truth, righteousness, faith, and remain in God's word so when hard times come you will be able to withstand. It is hard times right now. It's time to pray and stand on God's word. Now is the time for endurance. Activate your faith. Do not let anyone or anything disturb your peace. Keep trusting. Keep praying. Keep pushing.

Positive Vibes Only

PHIL.4:8 NIV

Finally, brothers and sisters, whatever is true, whatever is noble, whatever is right, whatever is pure, whatever is lovely, whatever is admirable—if anything is excellent or praiseworthy—think about such things.

New Hood Translation:

You are what you think. Be careful what you allow to consume your mind and your time. The word says as a man thinketh so is he.

Don't become overly consumed with the news but read the good news of the Lord. Limit yourself from talking with negative people. Be encouraged. It doesn't feel good right now but God is still good. Focus on the goodness of the Lord. Pull the plug on negative vibes.

Sandy N. Ward, M.ED

You ever talk to people and by the time the conversation is over you feel down? Negativity can pollute your atmosphere. Worry about

nothing and pray about everything. God got you! It could be better but it could be a whole lot worst. Keep trusting. Keep praying. Keep pushing!

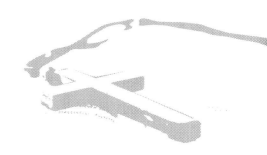

Tell of his goodness

1 PETER 3:15 NIV

But in your hearts revere Christ as Lord. Always be prepared to give an answer to everyone who asks you to give the reason for the hope that you have. But do this with gentleness and respect,

New Hood Translation:

Tragedy is surrounding us. Plague is present. Spirits are low. It is hard times but Lord our hope and trust is in you. Many are watching and listening to your response to life during these difficult times. They don't understand why you have peace. They don't get why your house is not lacking. We are not exempt from hard times. We will face difficult times but not in the same manner as the world. We have a covenant with God and because of that hedge of protection we must bear witness and tell of God's goodness. Don't beat people over the head with God's word but tell of his goodness, his protection, and his peace. Remember you maybe the only version of God that some may see. How do you represent Christ? Fear not, be of good cheer. Keep trusting. Keep praying. Keep pushing.

It's Not Time to Quit

1 CORINTHIANS 15:57 NIV

He gives us the victory through our Lord Jesus Christ. 58 Therefore, my dear brothers and sisters, stand firm. Let nothing move you. Always give yourselves fully to the work of the Lord, because you know that your labor in the Lord is not in vain.

New Hood Translation:

This is not the time to grow weary in well doing. It's not time to give up. Sometimes it feels like we are fighting a losing battle. This part of the journey is necessary for you to get to his promises. Don't be easily shaken. Stand boldly on the word of God. Put your best effort forward because your work will pay off. Don't let the present circumstances shake you. The storm is passing over but we can rest during the storm because he has already given us the victory! We are playing a game where the enemy has already forfeited. We are destine to win if you don't throw in the towel. Stand strong! Keep trusting. Keep praying. Keep pushing!

He paid the price

ISAIAH 53: 5 NIV

But he was pierced for our transgressions, he was crushed for our iniquities; the punishment that brought us peace was on him, and by his wounds we are healed.

New Hood Translation:

God knew we would fall short. He knew we would be drawn to sin. He foresaw the issues we would face in this world. He loved us so much that he gave his only son to be crucified so we could have peace. We are healed and have access to healing because of his

wounds. He got up from the grave with all power so that the issues we face in this world would never be bigger than God. Smile. Keep trusting. Keep praying. Keep pushing.

It's Only Temporary - Be Encouraged

ROMANS 8:18 NIV

I consider that our present sufferings are not worth comparing with the glory that will be revealed in us. 1 Peter 5:10 And the God of all grace, who called you to his eternal glory in Christ, after you have suffered a little while, will himself restore you and make you strong, firm and steadfast.

New Hood Translation:

Trouble doesn't last always. There will be glory after this. We thank God for the rain because it takes rain to

make things grow. Sometimes the rain is inconvenient, but it is necessary. Hard times are the same way in our lives. Hard times make us strong. It shows you what you are really made of. Some people fall apart and lose hope when it looks difficult. As children of God he has equipped us with everything we need to push through every difficult situation. It's not for you to understand. It's your responsibility to trust, obey, and pray. This too shall pass but it is part of the plan. Keep trusting. Keep praying. Keep pushing!

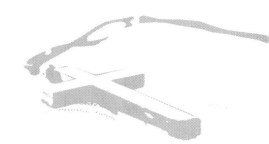

Love

Love is patient, love is kind. It does not envy, it does not boast, it is not proud. 5 It does not dishonor others, it is not self-seeking, it is not easily angered, it keeps no record of wrongs. 6 Love does not delight in evil but rejoices with the truth. 7 It always protects, always trusts, always hopes, always perseveres. 8 Love never fails.

New Hood Translation:

Love is not easy but the sanctity of marriage is ordained by God. It is a covenant between you, your spouse, and God. When you say I do, your issues, insecurities, and demons say we do too. You are accepting the other person with their flaws and issues. You are agreeing to put their needs first, to honor them, to protect them, and trust them. In marriage you don't just want someone to add value to you. You want some who can multiply you. You want someone to support your dreams, calm your doubts, someone you can trust, and someone who will cherish the opportunity to make you a better person. Communication is everything! Talk, laugh, and love. Make the memories that matter. Everyday will not be filled with sunshine but real love makes you spend your nights wanting to make the other person's days better. I pray that love may consume your union and you will love your spouse the way that God loves us with patience, forgiveness, unconditionally, and everlasting! Keep trusting! Keep praying. Keep pushing!

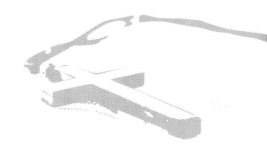

That's how strong my love is

ISAIAH 54:10 NIV

Though the mountains be shaken and the hills be removed, yet my unfailing love for you will not be shaken nor my covenant of peace be removed," says the Lord, who has compassion on you.

New Hood Translation:

Otis Redding sung a song in 1965 that said "I'll be the ocean so deep and wide And catch the tears whenever you cry I'll be the breeze after the storm is gone To dry your eyes and love you warm, That's how strong my love is. My husband used to sing the song like he wrote it. I could feel the lyrics. But God wrote the original version. He promised to never leave us nor forsake us. He promised to be a mother to the motherless. He promised when life around us was sinking sand and everything else failed us his love would still stand. That's how strong his love is! He is peace in the storm. He is a provider and a way maker. This too shall pass. God's love is bigger than our present circumstances. Keep trusting. Keep praying. Keep pushing!

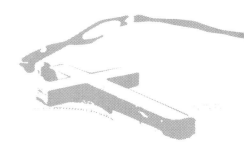

Worship outweighs worry

PSALM 118:1 NIV

Give thanks to the Lord, for he is good; his love endures forever.

New Hood Translation:

It's better to worship than to worry. Pause and tell God thank you. Thank you for life. Thank you for waking me up. Thank you for supplying all of my needs. Thank you for loving me when I didn't love myself. Thank you for health and strength. Thank you for blessing and protecting my family. Thank you for friends who have become family. Thank you for the hard times that come to make me strong. Thank you for breaking my heart so I would know you as a healer. Thank you that trouble doesn't last always. He keeps on making a way! Worship while you are waiting and watch God move. Keep trusting. Keep praying. Keep pushing.

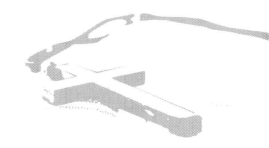

Do you believe?

MARK 9:24 NIV

Immediately the boy's father exclaimed, "I do believe; help me overcome my unbelief!"

New Hood Translation:

Where is your faith? Many times we believe in God but then doubt his capabilities. We know he has power but then doubt how his power can fix our circumstances. We pray to God, we praise God, but we run into hard times and doubt God. I will never forget my daughter was crying because she needed $5 for school and she was worried that I didn't have it. I asked her how will you know I don't have it if you never asked me. I told her about faith and how I had way more than $5 but she was missing out by doubting. Later that day I went to the doctor and they told me my husband's cancer treatment would be $200 a day plus medical expenses 3-5 times a week for the next upcoming weeks. I remember starting to cry and the Lord said but you did just like your child and doubted without even asking me. God has your answer he is just waiting for you to ask and BELIEVE. In

Mark 9 a man needed his son healed and Jesus told him it was possible if he believed. He responded that he believed but help his unbelief. What do you need help believing God for today? He won't fail. He has all power in his hands. What are you having faith that God will do? Keep trusting. Keep praying. Keeping pushing!

What About Your Friends?

PROVERBS 17:17 NIV

A friend loves at all times, and a brother is born for a time of adversity.

New Hood Translation:

Life brings about different seasons. Sometimes we are up and other times we are down. We experience joys and pains but a friend loves at all times. A friend will not turn their back on you when you face hard times. Loyalty in friendship is important. Hardships are lessened when a friend is there to comfort and help. A friend will be there to lift you up and not tear you down. You don't abandon a friend in difficult times. God sends people in our life for a reason. He sends us into the life's of others for a reason. Friends make mistakes. We all make mistakes. Be willing to forgive and offer support. Keep trusting. Keep praying. Keep pushing.

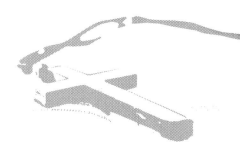

Do Not Get Tired Yet

ISAIAH 40:29NIV

He gives strength to the weary and increases the power of the weak.

New Hood Translation:

Sometimes our faith and hope can feel very low. It seems like we have taken all that we can take. It is in those times that you should push even harder. God rewards your diligence. He knows the load is heavy. When you call out to him and ask for help he helps you to get through it. The situation will not always disappear immediately. He will strengthen you to get through it. Why does God even allow difficult situations? It is in the dark times that you grow stronger in faith, patience, and endurance. You will find strength that you did not know you had if you just hold on. Keep trusting. Keep praying. Keep pushing.

It Does Not Matter

ROMANS 8:31 NIV

What, then, shall we say in response to these things? If God is for us, who can be against us?

New Hood Translation:

Who or what is bigger than God? There is nothing too big or too hard for God. It does not matter who or what you face because God is on our side. Nothing can stop you. Your future is in God's hands. There is no doctor's report bigger than God. There is no problem in your home or job bigger than God. The Lord will fight our battles. No weapon created to tear you down will work. God is with you. God is for you. Keep trusting. Keep praying. Keep pushing!

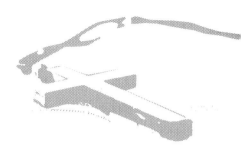

Encourage Someone

1 THESS. 5:11 NIV

Therefore encourage one another and build each other up, just as in fact you are doing.

New Hood Translation:

Take the time to check on someone. Let people know you are thinking about them, you love them, and they matter. The quickest way to lift your spirits when you are down is by offering words of encouragement to someone else. In difficult times you find many people to tell you to be strong and don't worry. Sometimes you need someone to say it is okay to not be strong right now. It is alright to hurt. It is cleansing when you cry. Uplift somebody and let them know you are not alone and it will get better. It is our job to build each other up. Stop frowning upon people facing hard times and offer encouragement. A smile, a listening ear, an offer of support goes a long way. Find someone to bless and watch your situation turn around. Keep trusting. Keep praying. Keep pushing!

76

He Loves Us

LAMENTATIONS 3:22 NIV

Because of the LORD's great love we are not consumed, for his compassions never fail.

New Hood Translations:

We are flawed but still favored. We have issues, insecurities, and shortcomings but God still loves us. Despite what we deserve he still loves us. God's love is beyond comparison. He gave his only son because he loved us. We fall short of his word but he still loves us. People will cut ties with you when they get tired of you. As ragedy as we are God still loves us. He provides for us. He supplies all of our needs. His mercies are new everyday because he loves us. Draw near to him and allow him to pour out his anointing over your life through his love. Keep trusting. Keep praying. Keep pushing.

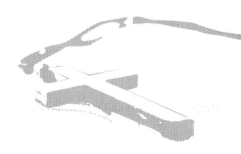

God Provides

PSALM 23:1 NIV

The Lord is my shepherd, I lack nothing.

New Hood Translation:

A shepherd is the leader of the flock. We have to choose to be followers of Christ. When we follow him all of our needs are meet. It does not mean you will have everything you want but you will have everything you need. He provides for us. He provides safety, hope, strength, and peace. God is bigger than just tangible things. He supplies all of our needs. He guides us in the right direction. He leaves a way of escape when we detour in the wrong direction. God is able. What you need seek him and he will provide. Keep trusting. Keep praying. Keep pushing!

Safe In His Arms

PROVERBS 18:10 NIV

The name of the LORD is a fortified tower; the righteous run to it and are safe.

New Hood Translation:

Because the Lord guides us we have everything we need. He takes care of his children. He allows us to rest during times of trouble. He gives us a safe place. When your faith is weakened, he offers strength. You do not have to search for a way out. He dispatches angels to see about you. In him there is no failure. When you run out of options run in to his arms.

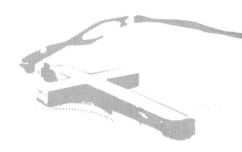

Carrying A Heavy Load

MATTHEW 11:28 NIV

Come to me, all you who are weary and burdened, and I will give you rest.

New Hood Translation:

God has the answer for you problem. Stop picking up the phone complaining to people who can not help you. You are looking for answers in the wrong place. The Lord said come to me. It is a burden to big for you to carry anyways. He would love to lift the weight off of your shoulders. It is no need for you to stay awake at night stressing over situations that you can not control. Pray about everything and worry about nothing. Give it to God and he will give you rest. Keep trusting. Keep praying. Keep pushing.

Be Grateful

I THESS. 5: 16-18 NIV

16 Rejoice always, 17 pray continually, 18 give thanks in all circumstances; for this is God's will for you in Christ Jesus.

New Hood Translation:

Stop complaining! Take the time in your prayer just to say thank you. We all have matters of the heart that we could petition before God. Sometimes we have to slow down and not request anything but just say thank you. Situations may not look favorable right now but thank God for being a way maker. You may not have everything you desire but thank God for being a provider. If he never does anything else he has already done enough. Put a smile on your face. Take joy in the simple pleasures. There are some phone calls that we dread answering because we know the person on the other end is going to be complaining or begging. God answers prays but he deserves our hallelujahs. God is good in spite of our present circumstances. Today take the time to just say thank you. Keep trusting. Keep praying. Keep pushing!

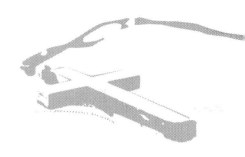

Be Obedient

DEUTERONOMY 11:1 NIV

Love the LORD your God and keep his requirements, his decrees, his laws and his commands always.

New Hood Translation:

Many times we find it easy to love the Lord but we struggle with keeping his commandants and trusting his word. I once told my daughter to go to the bathroom and take her pajamas and I would come and bathe her. Moments later she sat crying in the hallway. I asked her what her problem was and she said I am scared and you didn't come. My response was you never did what I told you. I was waiting for you to get your pajamas and go to the bathroom and then I would have done my part. I was never going to send her alone I just wanted her to follow my directions. Wow! Don't we do God the same way? Whining and waiting on him to change the situation but he gives us clear directions and we are too afraid to take the first step. He is never going to leave us but we choose to sit in darkness, misery, and defeat because we are afraid to make a move and follow his orders. If you want better, do better. Be obedient. Keep trusting. Keep praying. Keep pushing!

About the Author

Life has not always been easy but she knew with prayer, praise, and her faith in God she could face even the toughest situations. Sandy Ward is a native of Houston, Texas. Growing up she had no choice but to be strong because she was the only girl with three brothers. Sandy's parents worked in the field of education which helped prompt her love for children and passion to become an educator. Her grandfather and uncle were pastors and she grew up in a faith based house. Praying quickly became a part of her daily routine. She grew up not just in church but in the church's choir and endulged in God's word. She learned to push through some of life's toughest challenges by trusting God and standing on his word. When Sandy is not writing you can find her cherishing life with her children, friends, and family while offering encouragement to those around her.

Printed in the United States
By Bookmasters